Dedicated To:
Sarah & Tristin

Written By: Abigail Gartland

Hello, my name is St. Gabriel the Archangel!

An archangel is a leader of angels and has a very important job.

God gives all of His archangels different missions.

My mission is to help humans on earth.

I have helped many people, but my most important mission was to help a young woman named Mary to know God's plan for her.

I shared a message from God with Mary, "Hail, favored one! Th Lord is with you."

Mary was afraid, but I said "Do not be afraid, Mary, for you have found favor with God."

I told her that she would conceive a son and that she would name him Jesus.

Mary was chosen by God, and I knew that she was going to be the perfect mother to the baby, Jesus.

God's mission for me is to love and help the people on Earth.

When Jesus returns to Earth, I will blow my trumpet to let everyone know.

Do you want to be more like me?

You can celebrate my feast day with me on September 29th.

I am the patron saint of messengers

I pray for you every day of your life.

St. Gabriel, Pray for us!

pyright:

art: © PentoolPixie © LimeandKiwiDesigns
nsed purchased: 1/10/2024

About the Author

Abigail Gartland

I love the saints and I love my faith. The idea for sharing the stories of the saints with little ones came when my dear friend were expecting their first baby. I wanted to create something as unique and special as our friendship. Each book is dedicated to very special people and groups who have enriched my faith in different ways. I am blessed to write these stories and appreciate the unending support of my family and friends. When I am not writing, am a middle school teacher. I hope you enjoy these stories. I pray for each and every person who opens one of my books to learn more about the saints.

Abbie

www.ingramcontent.com/pod-product-compliance
Lightning Source LLC
LaVergne TN
LVHW050134080526
838201LV00120B/4910